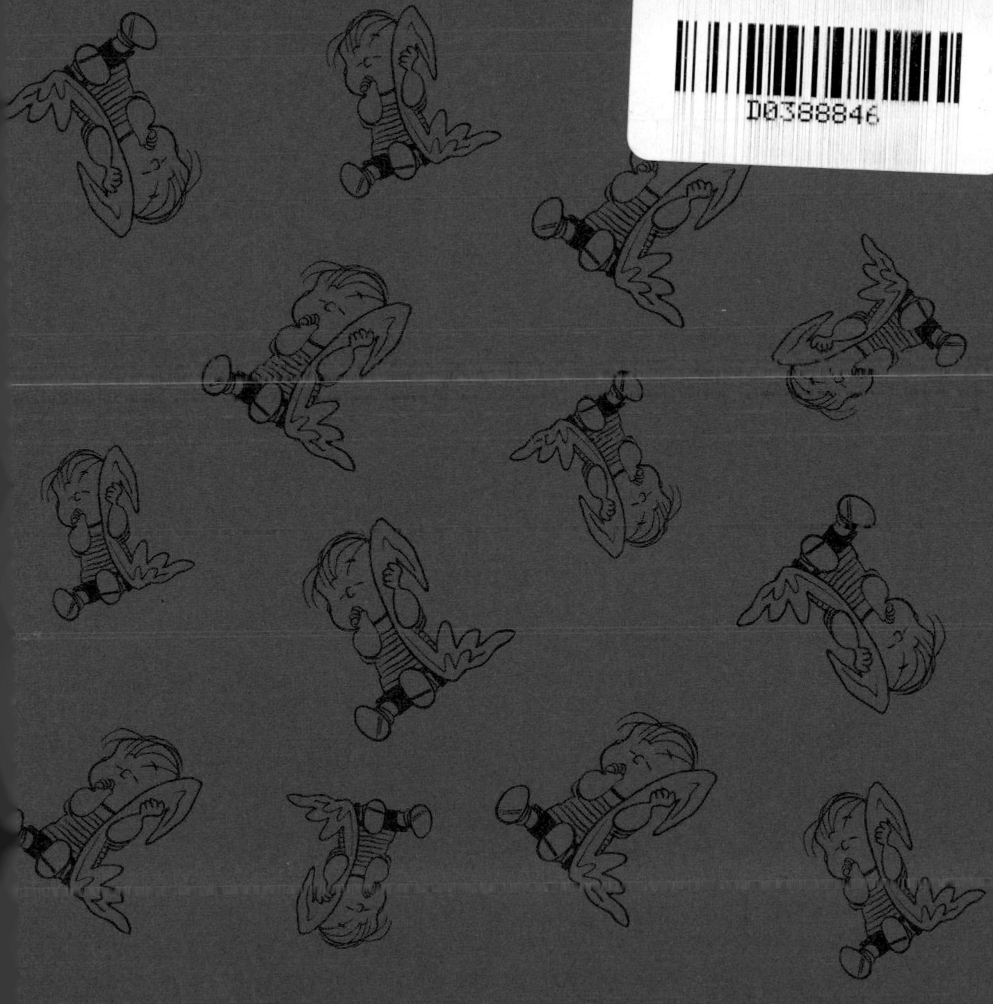

SECURITY IS A THUMB AND A BLANKET

BY
CHARLES M. SCHULZ

ISBN-13: 978-1-933662-09-1
ISBN-10: 1-933662-09-3

This book may be ordered by mail from the publisher.
Please include $4.50 for postage and handling.
But please support your local bookseller first!

Books published by Cider Mill Press Book Publishers are available at special discounts
for bulk purchases in the United States by corporations, institutions, and other
organizations. For more information, please contact the publisher.

Cider Mill Press Book Publishers
"Where good books are ready for press"
12 Port Farm Road
Kennebunkport, Maine 04046

Visit us on the web!
www.cidermillpress.com

Design by: Jason Zamajtuk

Printed in China

2 3 4 5 6 7 8 9 10

A PEANUTS CLASSIC Edition

SECURITY IS A THUMB AND A BLANKET

Security is having someone to lean on.

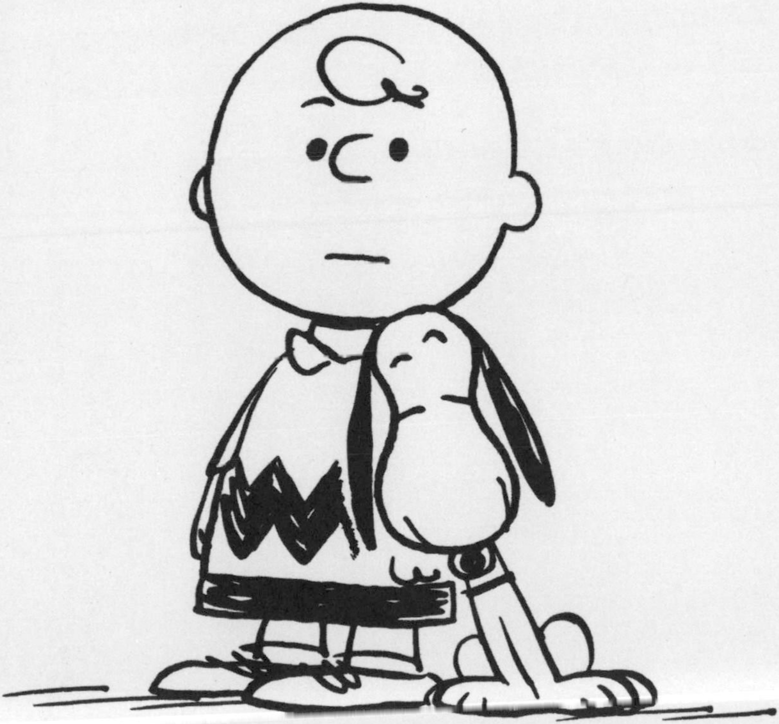

**Security
is knowing
you won't be
called on
to recite.**

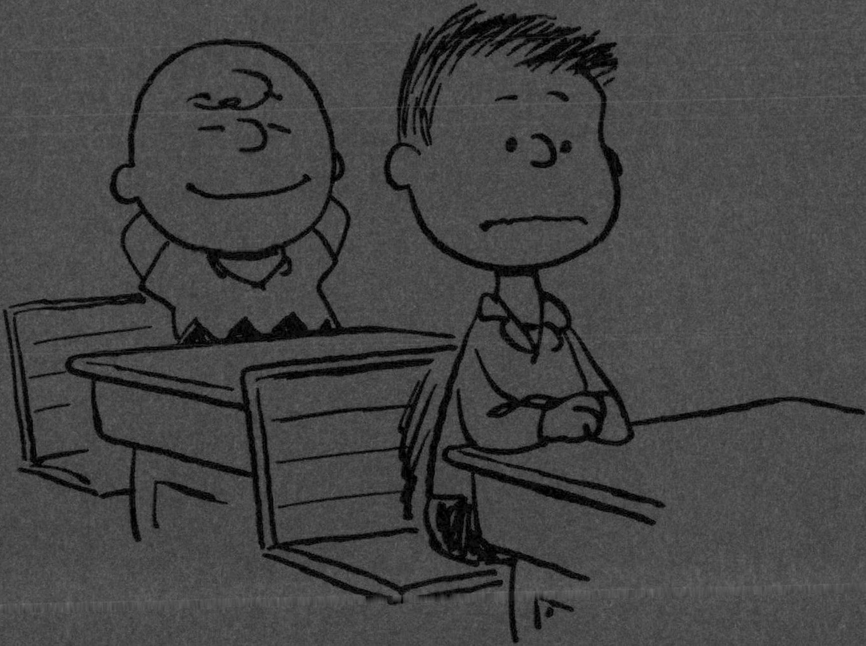

Security
is knowing
who the
baby sitter
is.

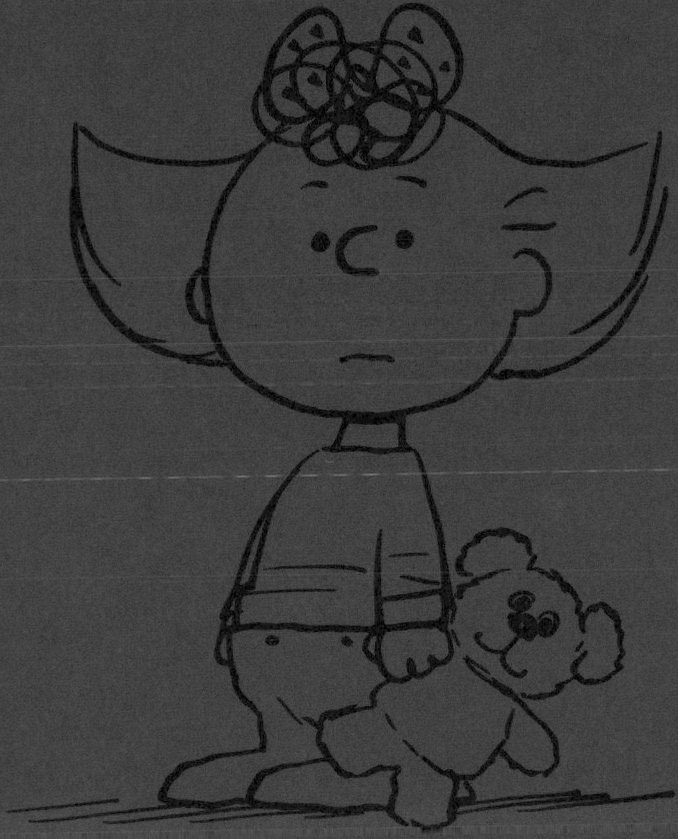

Security
is having
your socks
match.

**Security
is knowing
you still have
quite a few
years to go.**

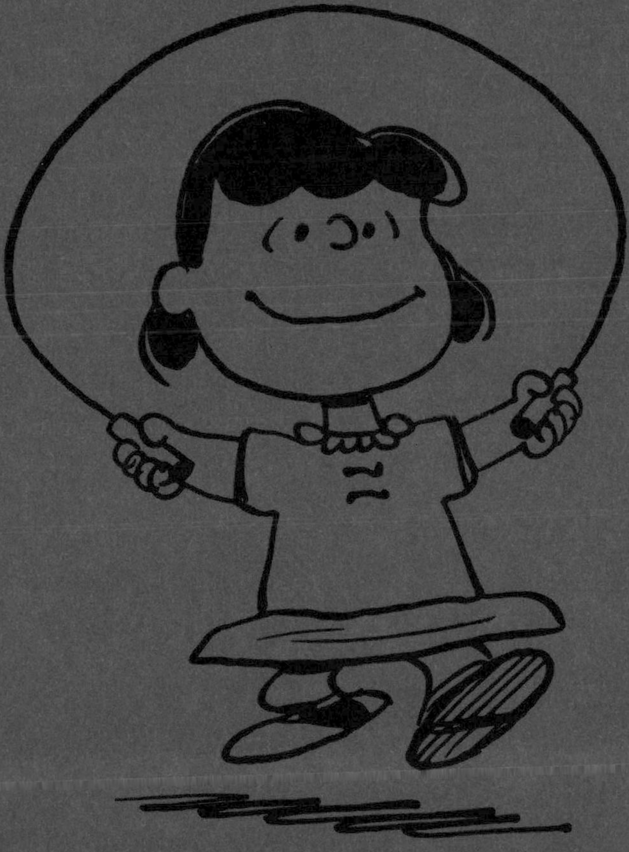

Security is owning your own home.

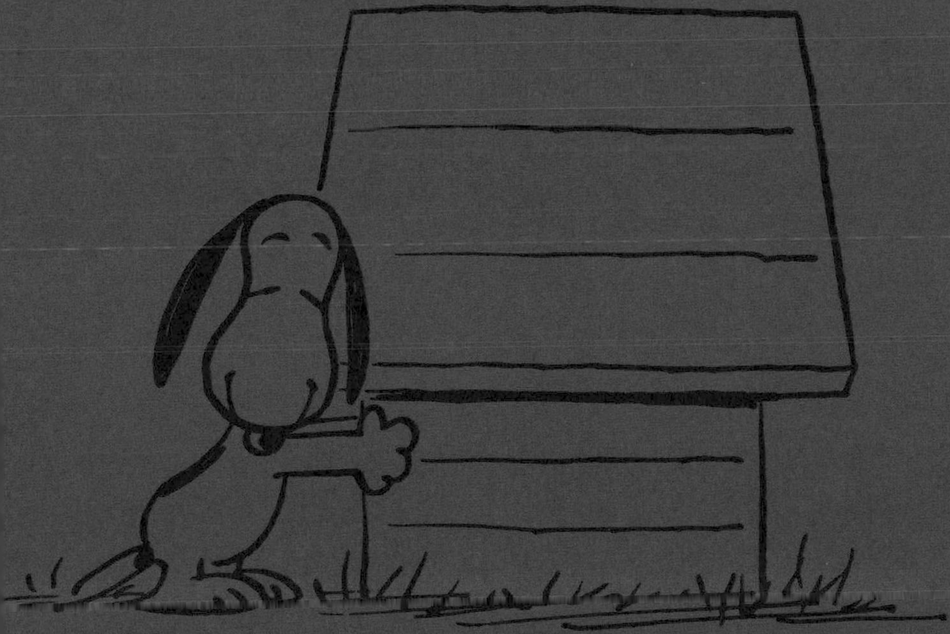

Security is having the music in front of you.

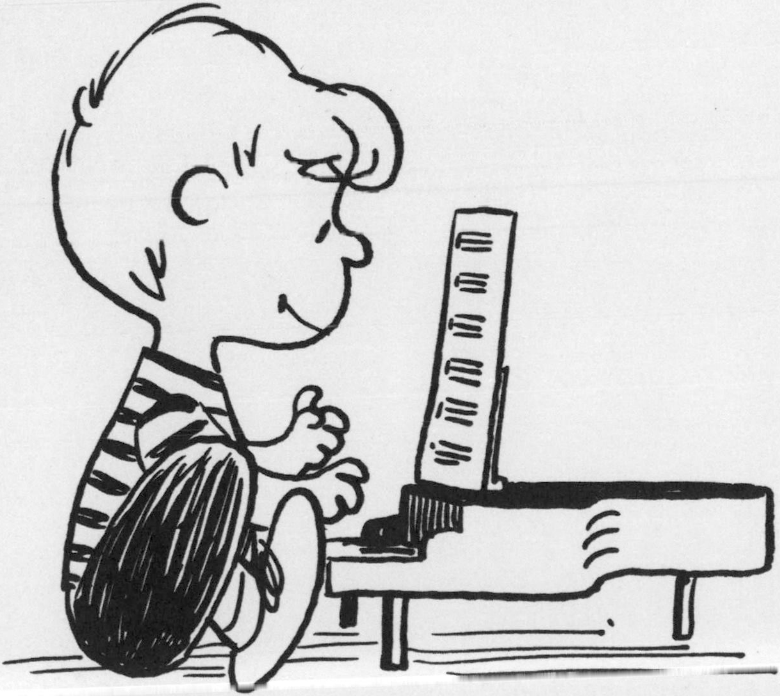

Security is having a big brother.

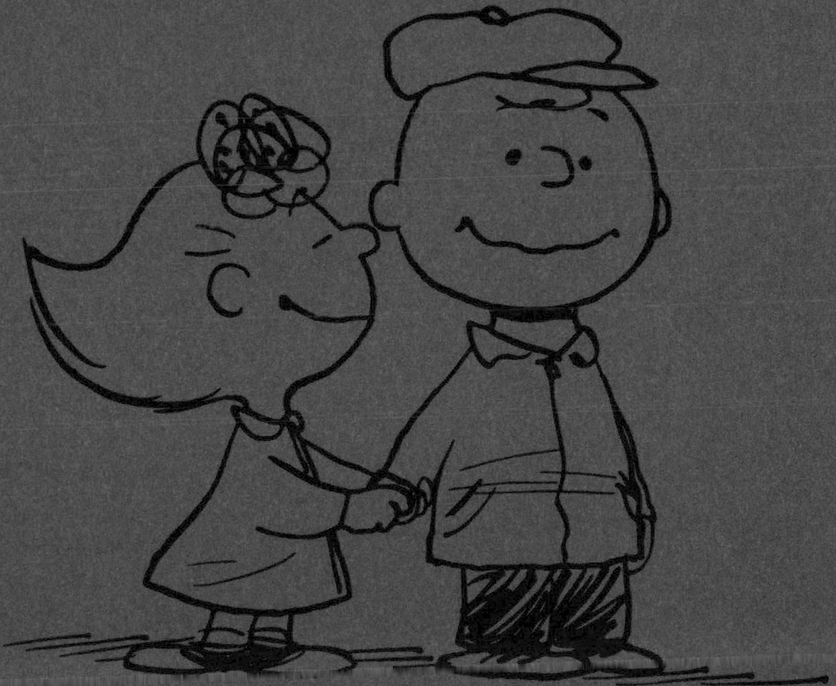

Security
is sitting
in a box.

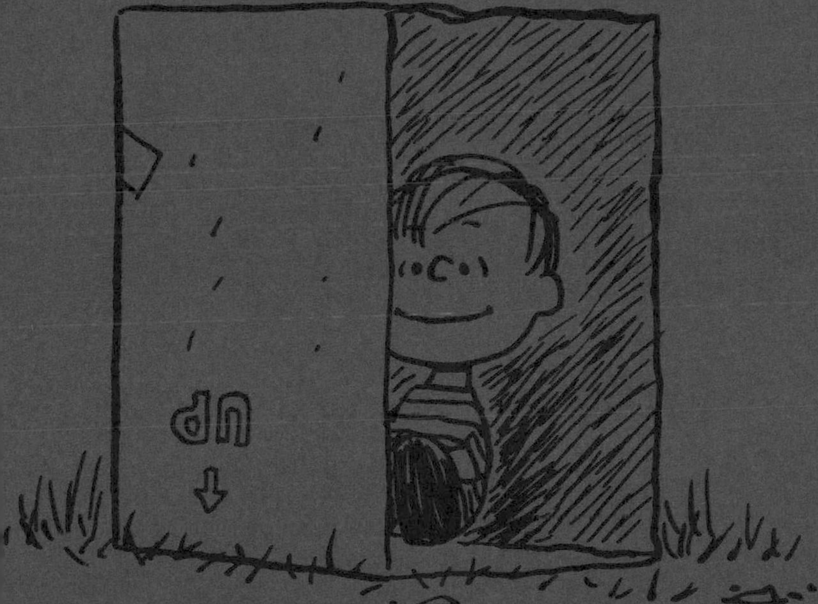
UP

**Security
is having a
good infield
behind you.**

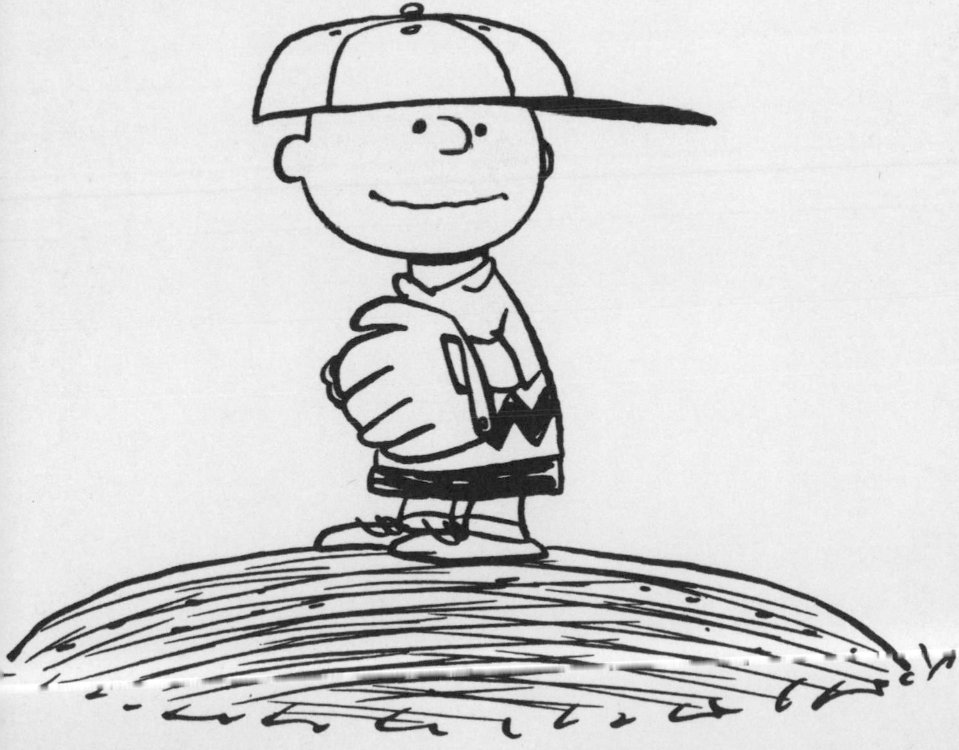

Security
is having
naturally
curly
hair.

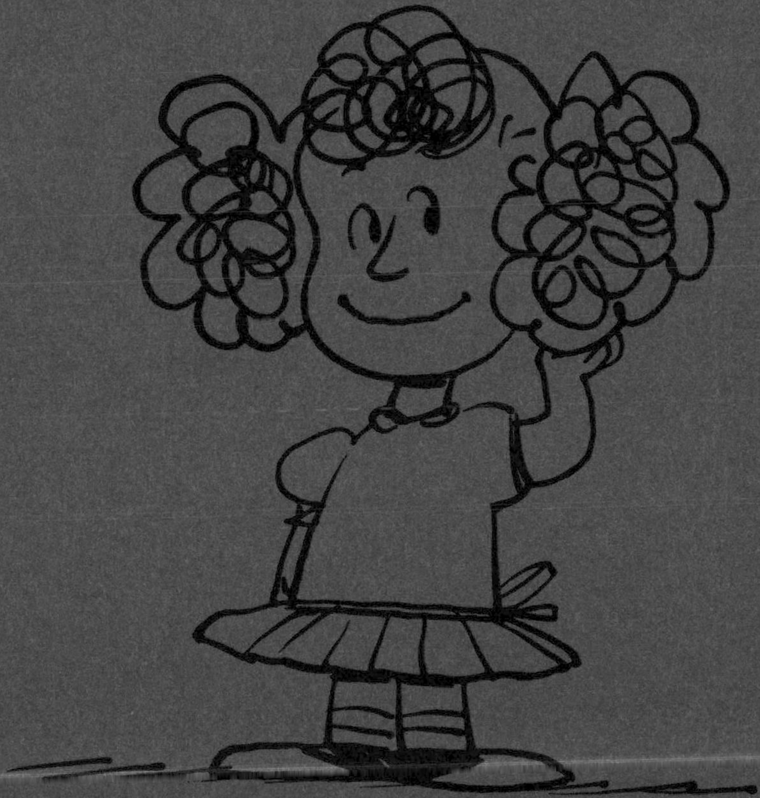

Security
is knowing
that big dog
can't really
get out.

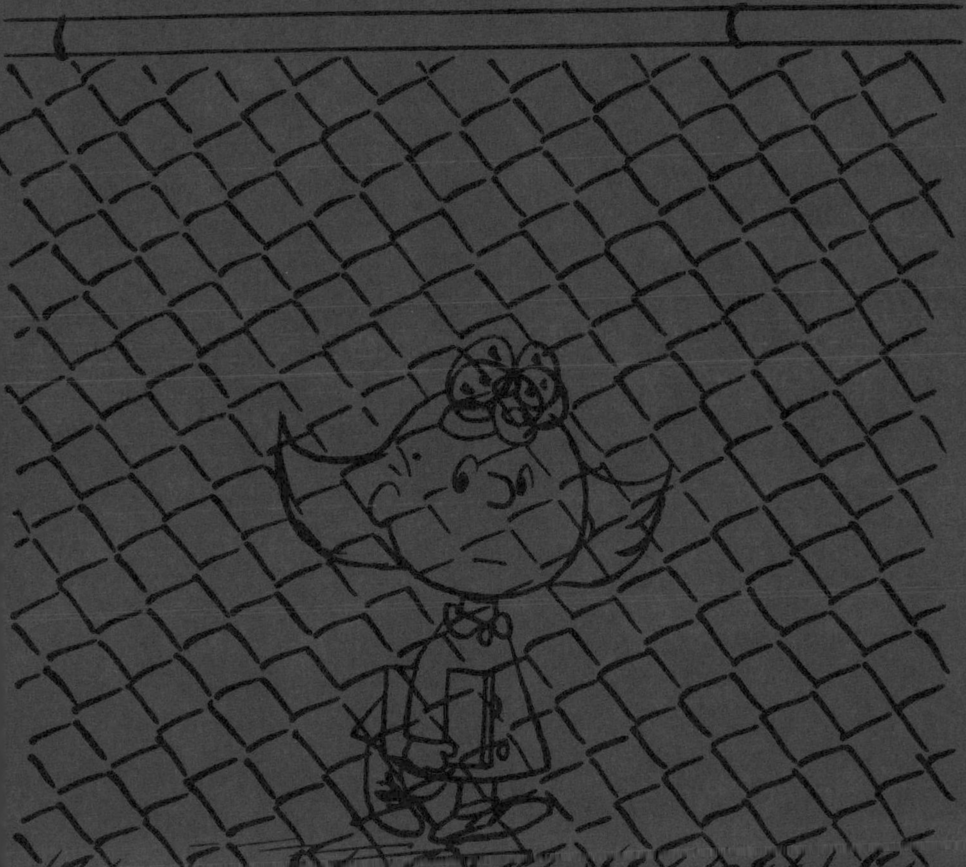

Security is having a few bones stacked away.

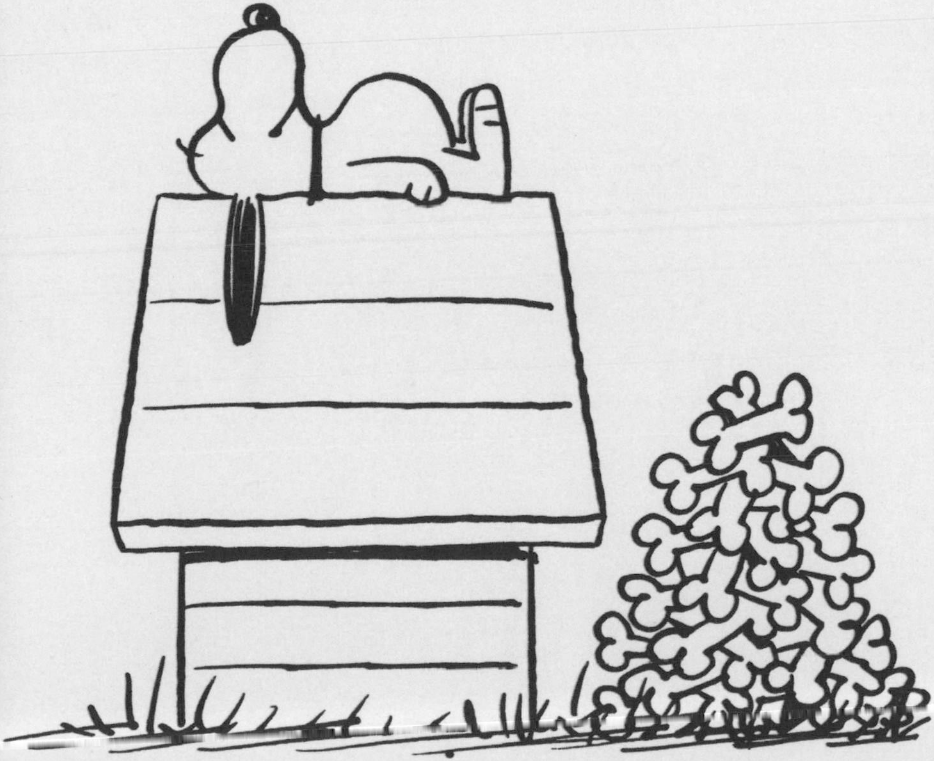

Security is holding the tickets in your hand.

Security is carrying an extra safety pin in your purse.

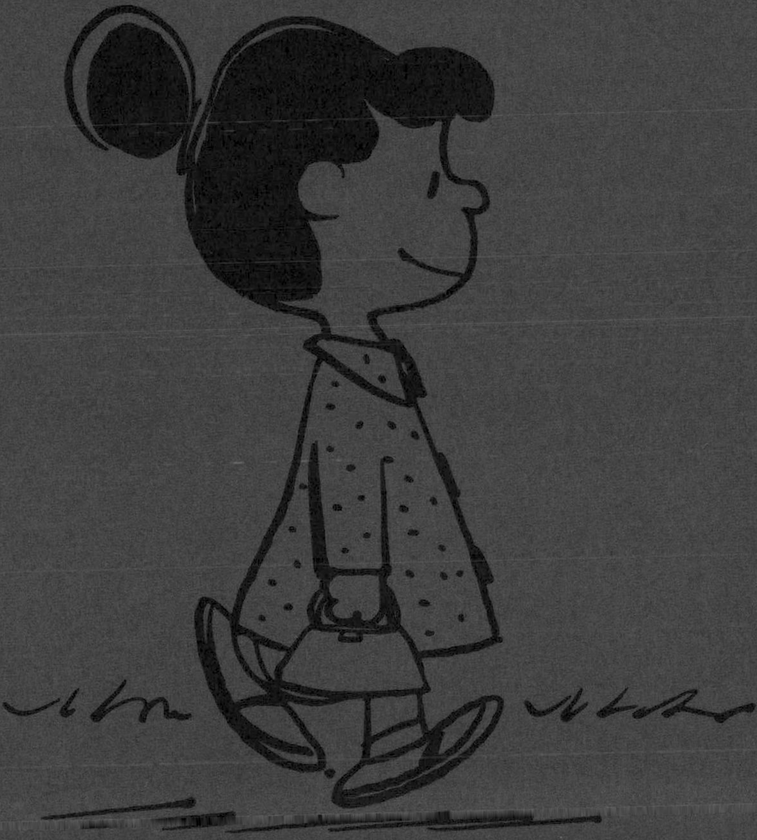

Security is writing down your locker combination.

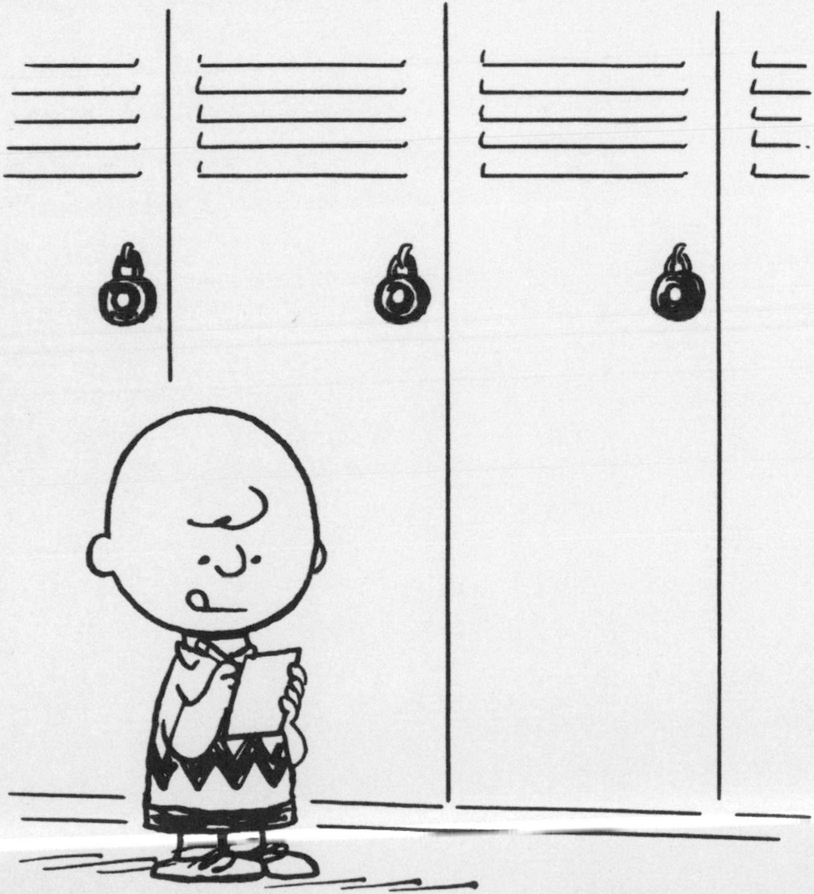

Security
is having
some friends
sleep
overnight.

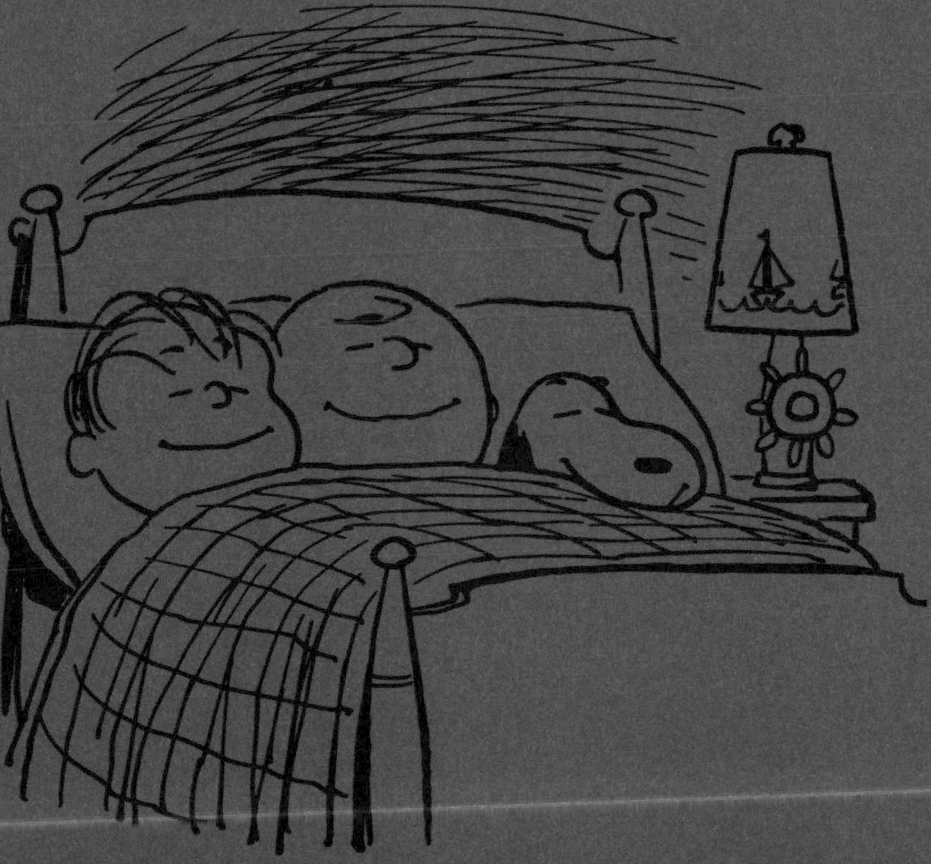

Security is being able to touch bottom.

Security
is giving
the mailbox
lid an
extra flip.

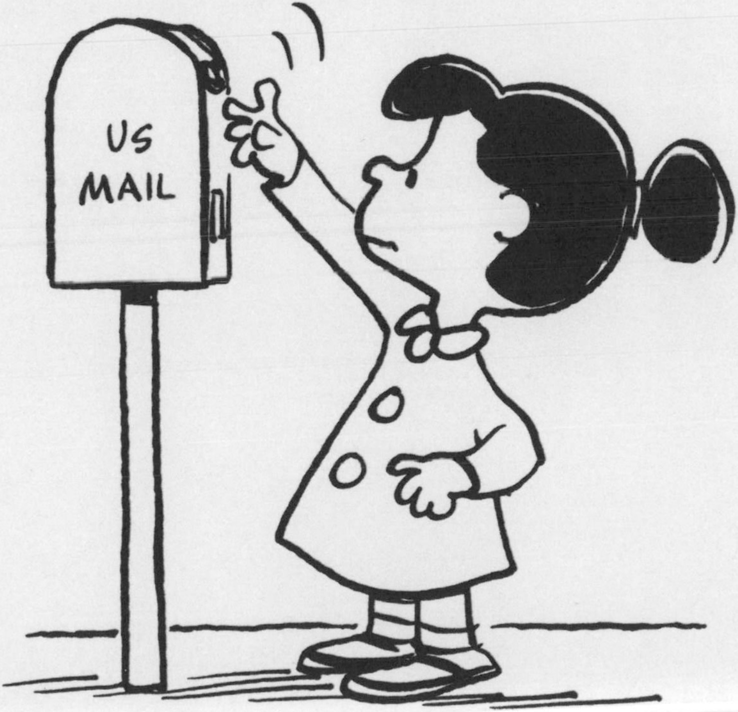
US
MAIL

Security is being one of the gang.

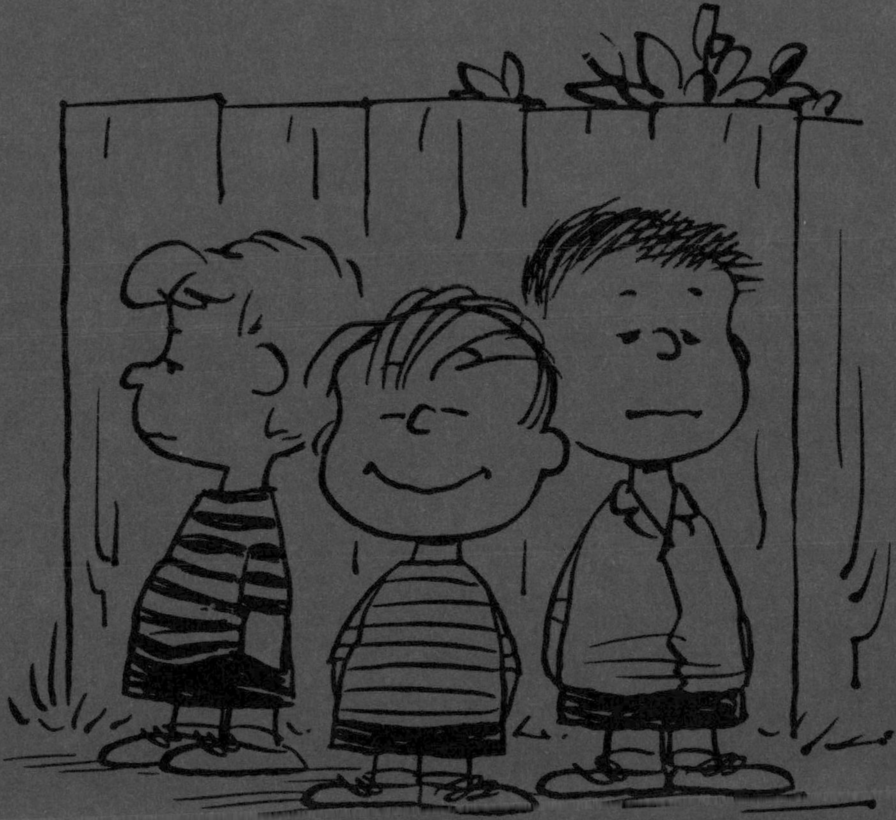

Security
is having
someone
listen
to you.

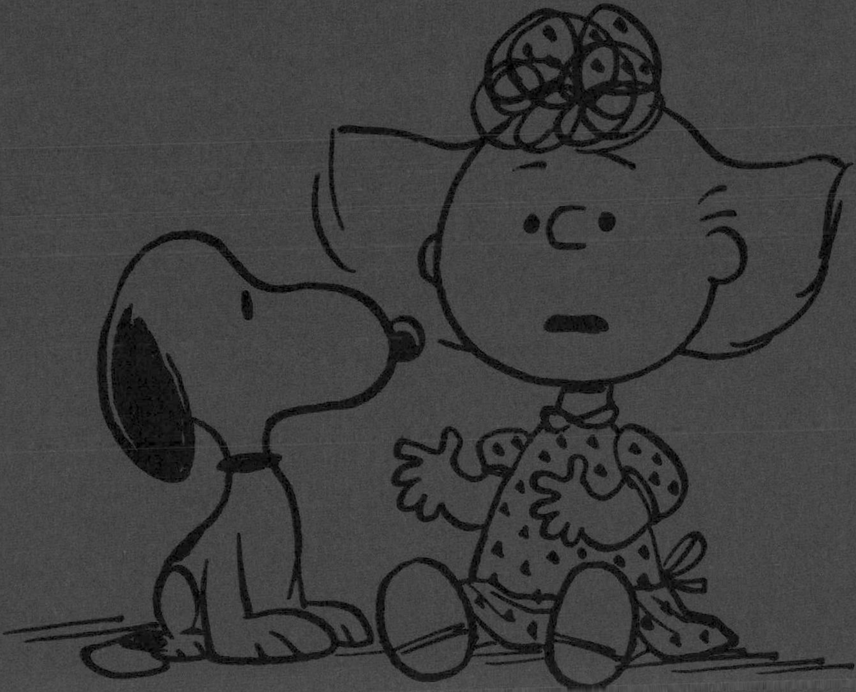

Security
is returning
home
after a
vacation.

Security is having a home town.

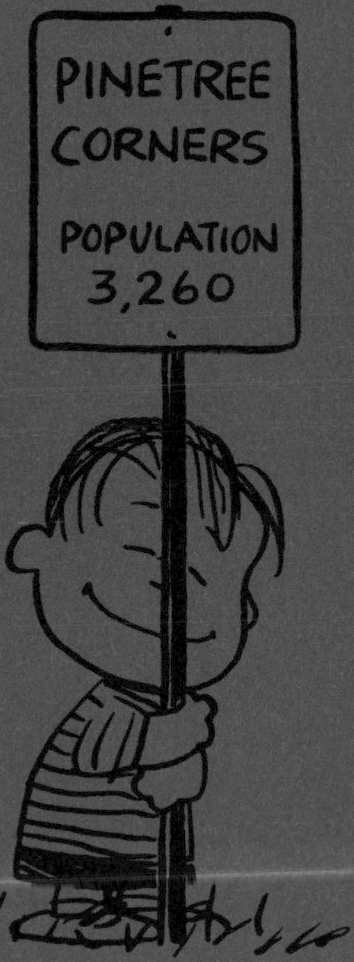
PINETREE CORNERS
POPULATION 3,260

Security is getting to the theater before the box office opens.

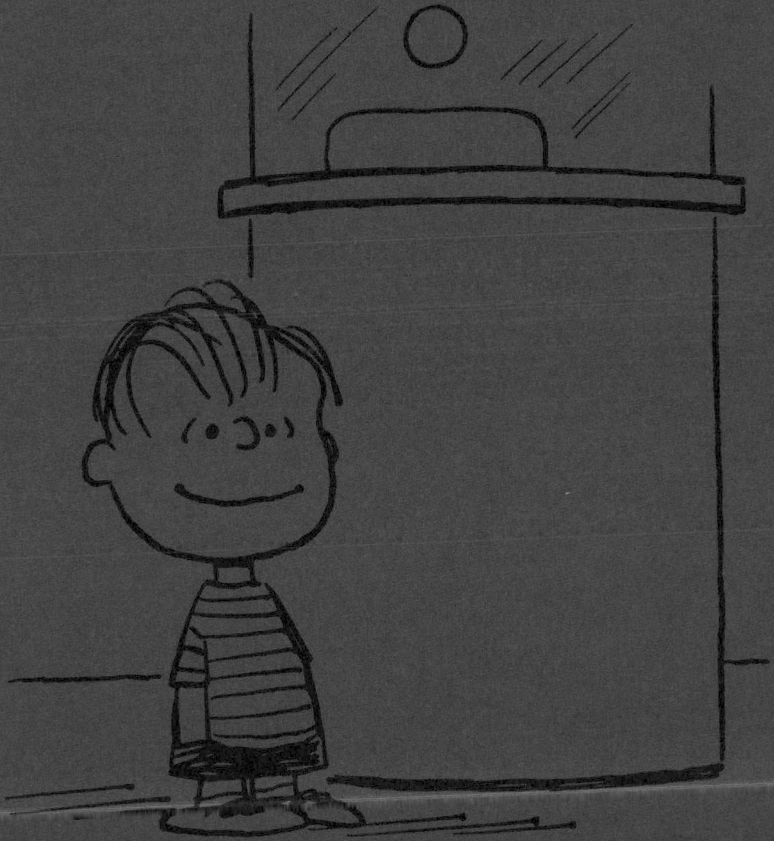

**Security
is knowing
there's
some more
pie left.**

Security is hiding an extra key to the back door.

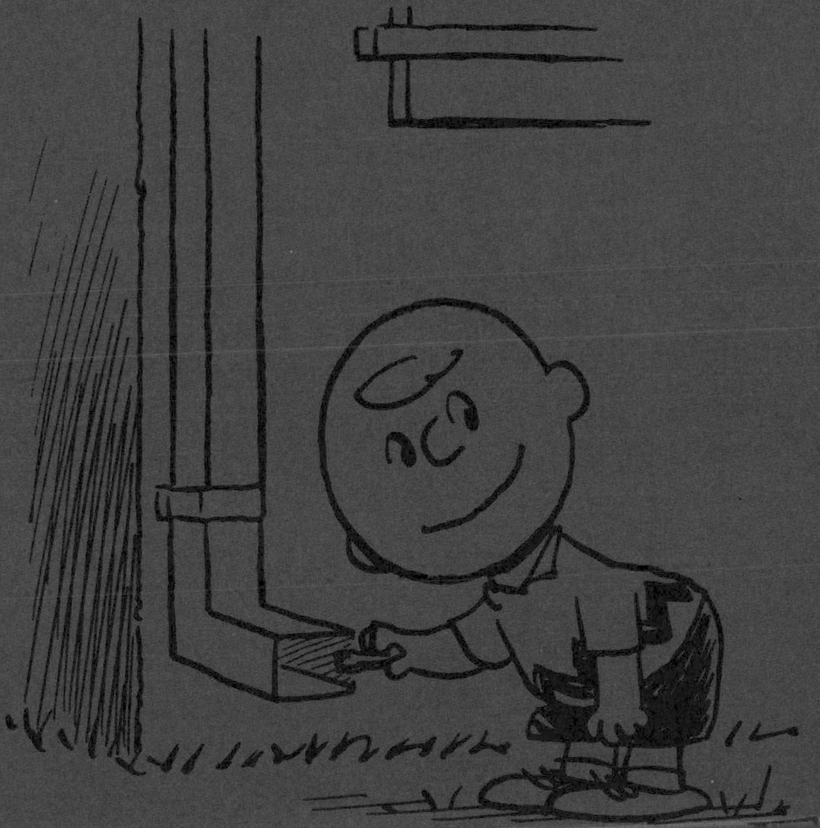

Security
is knowing
all your
lines.

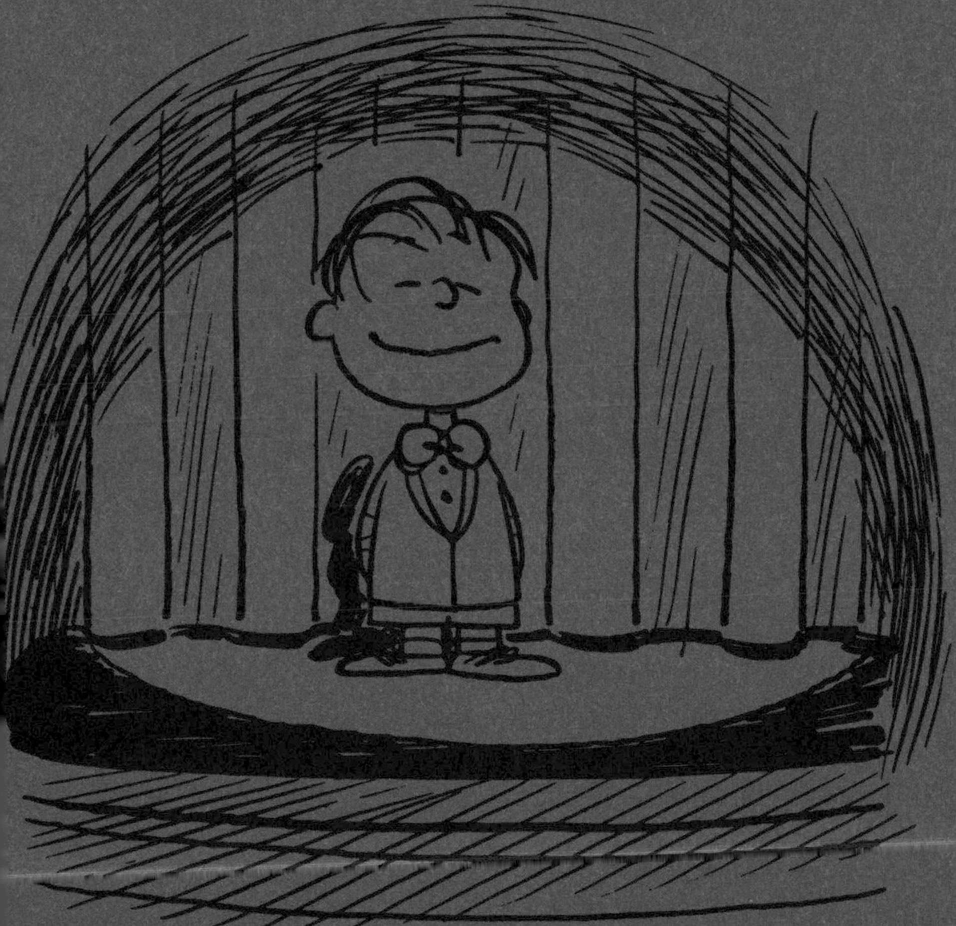

Security is a candy bar hidden in the freezer.

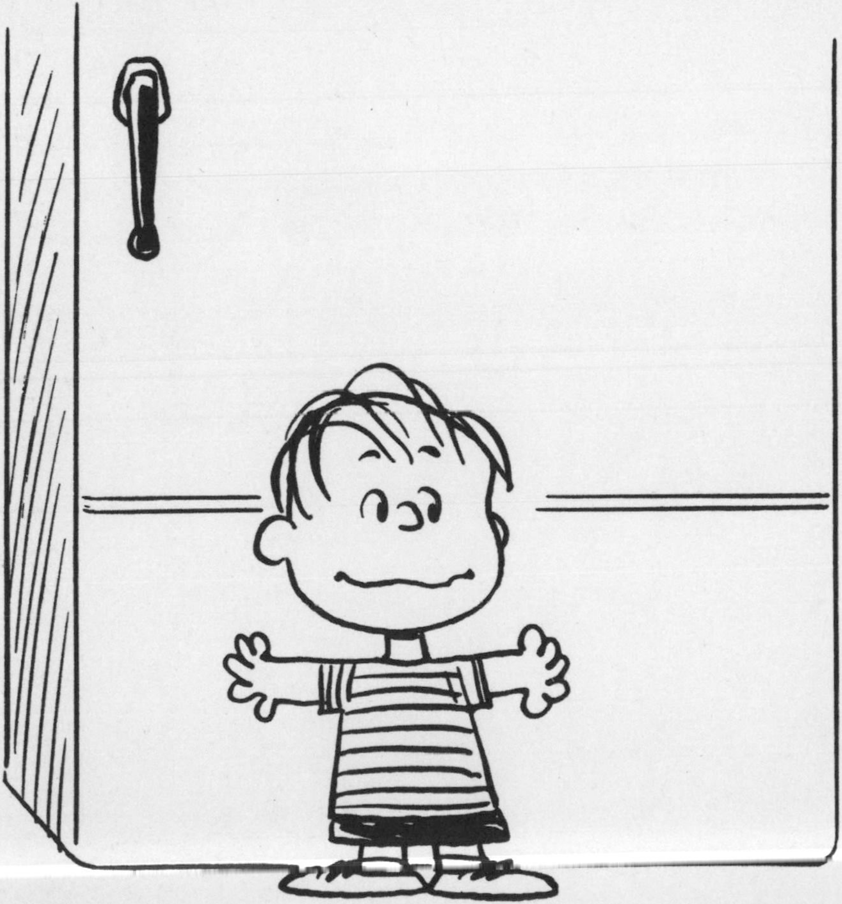

**Security
is hearing
your mother
in the kitchen
when you
come home
from school.**

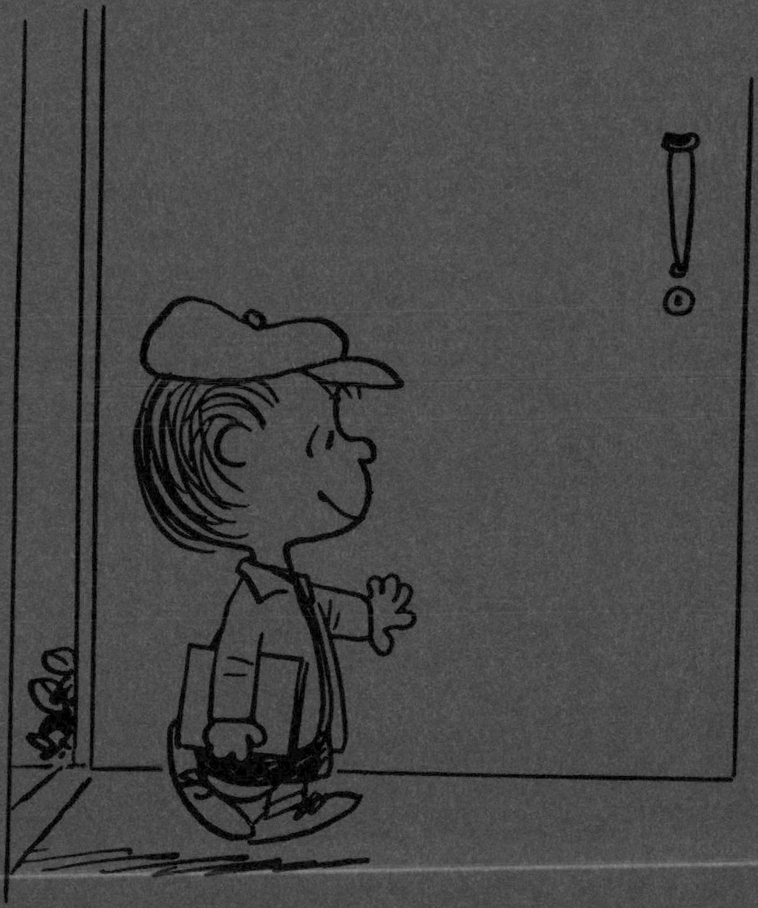
!

Security
is knowing
you're not
alone.

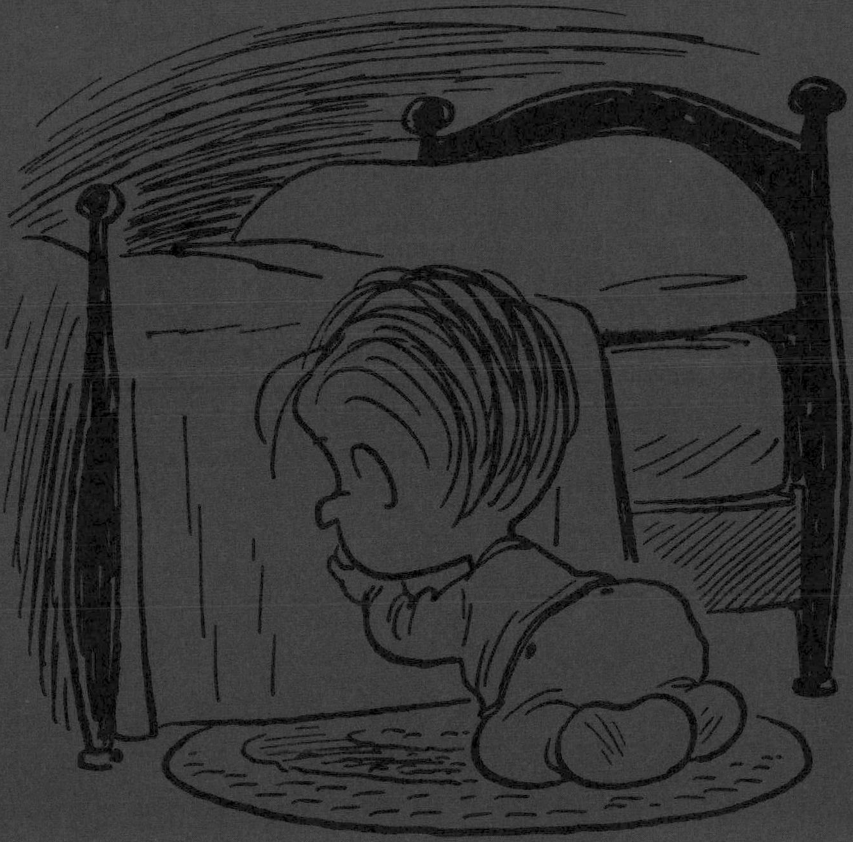

About Cider Mill Press Book Publishers

Good ideas ripen with time. From seed to harvest, Cider Mill Press strives to bring fine reading, information, and entertainment together between the covers of its creatively crafted books. Our Cider Mill bears fruit twice a year, publishing a new crop of titles each Spring and Fall.

Visit us on the web at
www.cidermillpress.com
or write to us at
12 Port Farm Road
Kennebunkport, Maine 04046

CIDER MILL PRESS
BOOK PUBLISHERS

Where Good Books are Ready for Press

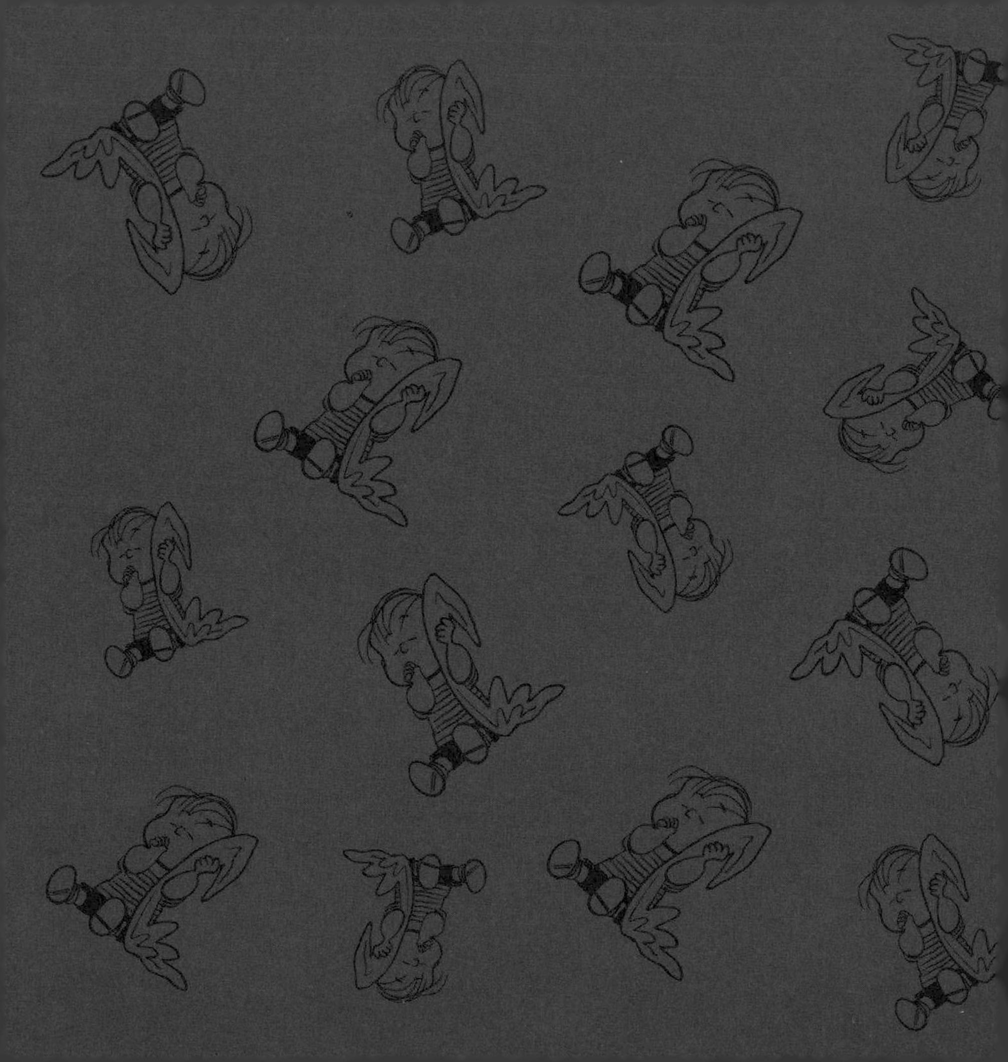